MY FAMILY REMEMBERS

The 1980s

James Nixon

W
FRANKLIN WATTS
LONDON • SYDNEY

Franklin Watts
This edition published in Great Britain in 2015
by The Watts Publishing Group

Planned and produced by Discovery Books Ltd., 2 College Street,
Ludlow, Shropshire, SY8 1AN
www.discoverybooks.net
Editor: James Nixon
Design: Blink Media

Dewey number: 941

ISBN: 978 1 4451 4356 9

Printed in China

Franklin Watts
An imprint of
Hachette Children's Group
Part of The Watts Publishing Group
Carmelite House
50 Victoria Embankment
London EC4Y 0DZ

An Hachette UK Company
www.hachette.co.uk

www.franklinwatts.co.uk

Words that are **bold** in the text are explained in the glossary.

Contents

Meet the families

The 1980s was a time of rapid change. The computer age was beginning. New luxury goods became available and for many it was a fun time to be young.

But the '80s was also a time of struggle for many, as old industries died and unemployment rose. Four children's families share their memories of those days.

Alice

Alice's family

Alice Hibberd is 13 years old. She has an older sister called Meg and lives with her mother, Julie, and stepfather, Tony. Lisa is Alice's older stepsister. She was born in 1971 and was aged between 9 and 18 in the 1980s.

Lisa

Sarah

Sarah's family

Sarah Hadland is 12 years old and lives with her older brother, Jacob, and parents, Marcia and Dan. Marcia was born in 1967 and was aged 13 at the beginning of the 1980s. Dan was born in 1971 and was 9 years old at the start of the '80s.

Dan

Marcia

Matty

Hazel

Matty's family

Matty Morris is 12 years old. He lives with his younger sister, Milly, his older brother, Peter, and his parents, Julie and Kevin. Julie and Kevin were teenagers in the 1980s. Peter's aunt, Karen, was born in 1967 and was 13 at the start of the decade.

Hazel's family

Hazel Stancliffe is 11 years old. She lives with her older sister, Lily, and her parents, Abigail and Paul. Abigail was born in 1967 and was aged between 13 and 22 in the 1980s while Paul was born in 1965 and aged between 15 and 24.

Julie

Kevin

Karen

Paul

Abigail

A changing world

Technology changed the way people lived and worked in the 1980s. High-tech goods, such as home computers, personal stereos, video recorders and the first mobile phones were new, exciting and in high demand.

People were encouraged to spend lots of money on luxury items and on looking good. Many city workers became very rich. These people were known as **yuppies**. They could show off their wealth by buying **designer clothes** and flash cars.

A wealthy city worker talks on her mobile phone.

Hazel asks her mum about life in the '80s: There was plenty of money around in the 1980s. I remember, even in poor areas, seeing groups of 'yuppies' looking posh, wearing their smart shirts, standing next to their fast cars and talking loudly.

But there were also large numbers of people who became less well off and found times difficult. Old industries, such as **mining** and shipbuilding, were shutting down and in parts of Britain thousands of jobs were lost.

The **unemployed** stand outside a job centre to protest against the loss of jobs in the early '80s.

Many people gave money to good causes to help the poor at home and abroad.

The Live Aid concerts in London and Philadelphia, USA, brought top music stars together and were shown on TV around the world. The event helped raise millions of pounds for the people starving in East Africa.

Alice asks her stepsister about Live Aid:
Live Aid in 1985 was one of the biggest events of the decade. I remember watching it in the front room with my family. I was glued to the TV as I waited in excitement for my favourite singers and bands to appear.

'I was glued to the TV.'

Life at home

The number of electrical items in homes increased in the 1980s. Many goods were becoming a lot cheaper. There were new-style plastic kettles and food processors that made cooking easier. Microwave ovens soon became common.

Sales of video recorders (VCRs) and video cameras grew quickly. Video recorders let you watch films on video cassette tapes which you bought or rented. You could also record TV programmes on to a blank video. There were no DVDs like there are today.

Hazel asks her mum about the gadgets in her home:

My mum was very proud of her big new food processor. She would show us the things it could do with dough and how to add stuff as you went along. But as time went on, it came out of the cupboard less and less often.

In the '80s people watched recordings on video cassettes like this one.

A Sony 'Betamax' video recorder, which played video cassettes loaded into the top of the machine.

The first home-video cameras went on sale in 1983. They were so bulky they had to be held on your shoulder.

It was not just films that were sold on cassette tapes – music was, too. The tapes could be listened to on large stereo systems or '**ghetto blasters**', or personal stereos that could be carried around.

This ghetto blaster has two tape decks at the front.

Computers were seen in the home for the first time in the 1980s. But they were usually only used for playing simple video games.

Three boys play a simple game on their home computer in 1983.

'**The graphics were very basic.**'

Sarah asks her dad how technology was different:

Some of my friends had a Betamax video recorder (opposite), which used cassettes smaller than the usual size. The remote control was attached to the end of a long wire!

My first computer was a Commodore 64. The games for this also came on cassette tapes and you had to wait about 25 minutes for each one to load! The graphics were very basic, but the games were great fun. I enjoyed playing *Manic Miner* where you had to find the flashing objects inside the caves.

Going shopping

The amount of money shoppers spent surged in the 1980s. There were lots of new products to buy and many people had plenty of money to spend. Shopping centres started to spring up everywhere.

Purchases of clothing soared. It seemed like looking good was more important than ever. Clothes, bags and shoes with designer labels were in high demand.

Acronyms were given to certain groups of people that had lots of money to spend in the '80s. Here are some in the box below.

Shoppers walk up and down a busy shopping centre in 1985. In the mid-'80s sales of goods were rising quickly.

Matty asks his aunt about food shopping:

We started using a large supermarket called Leo's to do our food shopping. Before that Mum had always used small stores such as bakers and butchers. We used to help Mum choose ready meals that could be cooked in our new microwave.

Yuppies – **Y**oung **U**rban **P**rofessionals
Woopies – **W**ell **O**ff **O**lder **P**eople
Dinkies – **D**ouble **I**ncome **N**o **K**ids
Poupies – **P**orsche **O**wning **U**rban **P**rofessionals

The number of supermarkets continued to grow in the '80s. Shoppers liked the huge number of goods they offered and their low prices.

In 1987, for the first time, customers could pay for goods at the till using a plastic debit card. The card took money from your bank account electronically. This was easier and quicker than writing a cheque or carrying lots of cash around.

Sarah asks her mum about shopping in the '80s: People seemed to want it all in the '80s. Even if you couldn't afford something you could buy it with a **credit card**, where you paid later. I remember all the TV adverts for credit cards, especially the Access card advert. On the advert the card turned into a cartoon character and called himself 'your flexible friend'.

The Access credit card was given arms, legs and eyes in this 1980s TV advert.

Leisure time

Computers, videos and stereos provided more entertainment in the home than ever before. The number of television programmes you could choose from also continued to grow in the '80s.

Channel 4 went on air for the first time in 1982. Then the BBC began to show programmes through the whole day in 1986.

In the '80s, US action-adventure show *The A Team* was very popular. In the team were: Murdock (top), B A Baracus (right), Hannibal (bottom) and Face (left).

Sarah asks her dad what he watched:

The A-Team was a series about a group of ex-soldiers. I thought it was great fun because it was full of comedy and action. But no one ever got hurt – even if thousands of bullets were being fired in all directions!

'It was full of action but no one ever got hurt.'

Some of the soap operas we watch today began in the 1980s, such as *Eastenders* and *Neighbours*. On Christmas Day 1986, *Eastenders* was watched by over 30 million people! Police dramas *The Bill* and hospital drama *Casualty* were also launched in the decade. The comedy *Only Fools and Horses* was a big hit.

For children, Saturday morning TV was a must-watch. *Going Live* presented by Phillip Schofield, Sarah Greene and Gordon the Gopher featured celebrity guests, competitions and cartoons. The '80s had some famous animations, such as *Thomas the Tank Engine*, *Postman Pat*, *SuperTed* and *Dangermouse*.

Phillip Schofield sits with his puppet Gordon the Gopher and presenter Sarah Greene on the set of *Going Live*.

Sarah asks her mum what her favourite TV show was:
American soap *Dallas* was my favourite show. 'Who Shot JR?' was a big storyline. I remember the news showing the reels of videotape being flown into the UK. They had to be guarded by security guards so no one could find out who did shoot JR before it was shown on television!

The Sony Walkman personal stereo was released in 1979 and became one of the most popular gadgets of the 1980s.

Many people were worried they were not getting enough exercise. A fitness craze took off in the '80s and leisure centres started to open up in many towns. It was common to see people out jogging while listening to a personal stereo at the same time.

Toys and crazes

In the 1980s there were many toys that made a big impact. The yo-yo, football stickers and the strange Rubik's cube were just some of the **crazes** that took hold.

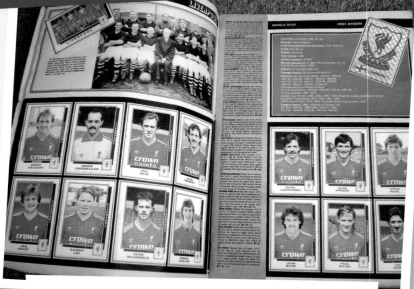

Collecting football stickers and swapping them with your friends was a craze in the mid-'80s.

The Rubik's cube was an almost impossible puzzle to solve, but over 200 million were sold!

Alice asks her stepsister about the Rubik's cube:

I did have a Rubik's cube, but it was my sister who was the whiz-kid on it. You had to match up the colours on each side of the cube. I used to run out of patience with it very quickly.

The Cabbage Patch Kids were a group of dolls, each with their own name and look. They became so popular that shops started to run out of them. Later in the decade, Sylvanian Families were all the rage. They were families of rabbits, frogs, mice and other animals.

Parents queue to buy their children Cabbage Patch Kids just in time for Christmas in 1983.

For boys, action figures were in high demand. Teenage Mutant Hero Turtles and He-man were based on TV cartoons. Transformer toys were also popular. They were robots that could be turned into vehicles.

Some outdoor toys became crazes. BMX bikes and skateboards were so popular in the 80s that they became professional sports.

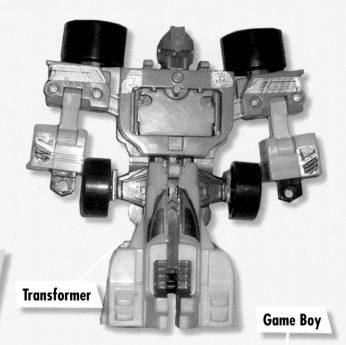

Transformer

Game Boy

Matty asks his dad about having fun:
I used to ride my BMX everywhere and every day. It was a *PK Ripper* (below) made out of aluminium. I even used it on my paper round. Me and a group of other boys built a BMX track in a friend's garden and used to race around it.

It was also the decade that electronic toys took off. Nintendo released its first games console in 1985. Then in 1989 came the Nintendo Game Boy, a handheld games system.

'I used to ride my BMX everywhere.'

Matty asks his mum about the games she played:
I had a handheld electronic game called Frogger – like a mini arcade game, which I loved. You had to get the frogs across a busy main road. It was the only computer game we owned!

Watching films

Now that families could rent or buy films on video, fewer people were going to the cinema. The video market **boomed** however.

Many films in the '80s made the most of the new computer technology and special effects that were possible. In *Back to the Future* (1985) Marty McFly the skateboarding teen goes time travelling in the DeLorean **supercar**. It was a huge success.

Marty McFly (left) looks amazed as the DeLorean supercar vanishes back in time.

Sarah asks her mum about watching videos:
Our local cinema closed down in the '80s. We started renting videos from the new video shop. Friday night was our video night and we would buy popcorn as well or try to make it ourselves!

The number of video shops grew quickly in the 1980s.

The trend for film **sequels** that we see today began in the '80s. There were further *Back to the Future* films and *Star Wars* sequels, such *as The Empire Strikes Back* (1980) and *Return of the Jedi* (1983). The *Indiana Jones* trilogy spanned the decade. The films followed Jones's search for ancient treasures as he battled past snakes, bottomless pits and giant, rolling boulders!

TIME DIFFERENCE

Going to the cinema was not as fashionable in the '80s as it had been in the past or is today. In just five years cinema visits had halved to 54 million in 1984. Today, there are around 170 million cinema visits each year.

One of the most popular children's films of the decade was *ET The Extra Terrestrial* (1982), the story of a loveable alien who was stuck on Earth.

ET, the famous alien from the film, points with his glowing finger.

Hazel asks her mum what films she liked:

ET made a big impression on me. Me and my friends were always singing the theme tune and saying the film phrases, such as 'phone home' pointing our fingers in the style of ET.

'Me and my friends were always pointing our fingers in the style of ET.'

Sounds of the '80s

In the 1980s, most people listened to music on small, portable cassette tapes. But cassettes had a problem – the tape would often tangle up in the machine and get damaged (right). CDs started to replace cassettes later on in the decade.

In 1981, the music television channel (MTV) was launched in the USA. It played artists' music videos 24 hours a day! For the first time, musicians had to think about recording a video as well as a song. Having a cool video was a good way to improve an artist's image.

TIME DIFFERENCE

In 1989, 15 per cent of households had a CD player. Now it is over 90 per cent!

Matty asks his mum about the music she listened to:

Madonna and Wham! were my favourites. I had a mirror in my bedroom with George Michael's face on it. Madonna pictures were plastered all over my wall. I had all the songs and played them constantly.

Pop bands such as Duran Duran and Wham! set their videos in exotic locations. The Wham duo (above) was made up of George Michael (left) and Andrew Ridgeley (right).

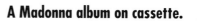

A Madonna album on cassette.

Michael Jackson was one of the most popular artists in the 1980s. He made the video an art form with his dance moves, such as the 'robot' and 'moonwalk'.

Michael Jackson dances in his video for the 1983 hit single *Billie Jean*.

A lot of '80s pop music had an electronic sound produced by new instruments such as the latest **synthesisers** and drum machines. But music was varied in the '80s. **Hip hop** and **heavy metal** became popular styles of music.

Sarah asks her dad what music he liked:
I was really into heavy metal in the 1980s. I went to my first ever concert to see Iron Maiden at the Birmingham Odeon. The ticket cost £6.50. It was a new experience for me – the lights, the smoke effects and the sound were all amazing!

Sarah's dad dressed up and ready to go to a heavy metal concert.

Power dressing to sportswear

One of the most popular looks for women in the 1980s was 'power dressing'. This meant wearing jackets or full suits in bright colours and with big shoulder pads. It made women look wealthy and successful.

Some people tried the 'new romantic' look which was often seen in nightclubs. They would dress as fantasy characters, such as pirates. Even men would wear bold make-up and clothing with lots of ruffles and frills.

Many women in the '80s dressed in suits that made them look successful and serious.

A group of teenagers dress in the style of new romantics. The make-up makes it difficult to tell if they are male or female.

Sarah asks her mum about '80s fashion:

Here is a picture of me (below) wearing a jacket with shoulder pads. Women had big hair in the '80s, too. I had a curly perm. I used gel to make it wet and Ultra Sheen hairspray to make it shiny and give it loads and loads of volume!

There were some interesting hairstyles in the '80s. One popular style was the 'mullet' – short hair on top and long hair at the back. To gain **street cred** it was important to have the right logo on your clothes. Children would often demand that parents buy them expensive items, such as trainers, with designer labels.

Here is Alice's stepsister with a 'mullet' haircut in 1985.

Sportswear became very fashionable in the '80s. Trainers, tracksuits, leggings, leg warmers and cycling shorts fitted in with the fitness craze of the time. Shellsuits were light, silky tracksuits in very loud colours.

Leotards, leggings and headbands came in bright, neon colours and were all part of the '80s fitness and dancewear trend.

Hazel asks her mum about dancewear:
My eldest sister used to make leg warmers by cutting the arms off her jumpers. Then she would have a sleeveless jumper, too!

'My sister used to make leg warmers.'

Schooldays

There were major changes in schools in the 1980s. In 1987, a new exam system was introduced for 16-year olds. GCSEs replaced the old O levels and CSEs. The GCSEs gave pupils more coursework as well as exams at the end of the two years.

Physical punishments such as caning and the slipper were banned in 1986. In 1988, the National Curriculum was introduced. This document told all state schools what subjects should be taught and how.

Matty asks her mum about exams:

I sat GCSEs when they first came out in 1987. It was a bit of a trial run. Both the children and the teachers were not quite sure what they were supposed to be doing!

TIME DIFFERENCE

In 1988, there were around 2,000 middle schools for children aged 8-12. Today, there are less than 300 and most children go straight from primary to secondary school.

Matty's mum at primary school.

Alice asks her stepsister about life at school:

Here is a picture of me (far right) at secondary school in the late 1980s. We often had to share textbooks because there was a lack of resources at the time. I played clarinet in the school orchestra and I remember playing for the Queen when she visited in 1989.

ERENCE BOOKS

NON FICTION

Most school research was done using books from the library.

'There were just two computers in the whole school.'

Computers were introduced into schools in the '80s, but they were only used for very simple tasks. The Internet was mainly used by scientists – there was no World Wide Web or search engines like there are now, so you could not use computers for research. Classrooms were quite old fashioned compared to today. Most still had blackboards and old wooden desks.

Sarah asks her dad about computers in school:
I remember that there were just two computers in the whole school. They were BBC Micros and they were locked away in a special room. The keyboards were very bulky and solid, which was good because it meant it was impossible for kids to break them!

At work

Many people earned huge amounts of money in the '80s working in city banks. They worked very long hours, but could afford luxurious lifestyles.

There were new accessories that became very popular among '80s workers. Mobile phone technology was just beginning. The first mobiles were very heavy and had a long aerial. The Filofax was a brand of personal organiser which became a must-have (below).

A worker's mobile phone was almost the length of a briefcase!

Hazel asks her dad about mobile phones: I got my first mobile phone in the '80s – it was absolutely huge! The battery needed charging every night and there was never any signal!

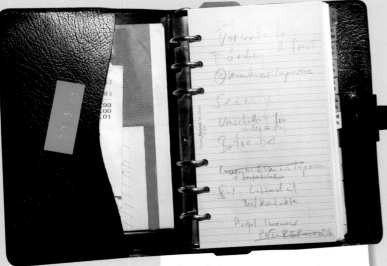

The Filofax was extremely popular as electronic organisers did not exist.

In the office, electronic word processors replaced the old typewriters. Computers started to appear and made some jobs easier. They could handle data and calculations but they were much slower than today. There were no emails then – instead workers used **fax machines** to instantly send letters and other documents around the world.

Sarah asks her mum about her job:
I started work in 1987 as a childcare officer. The computers we used were very basic compared to those of today, but at the time we thought they were cutting edge.

'We thought they were cutting edge.'

An early Apple computer from the 1980s.

The National Union of Mineworkers went on many strikes to protest against job losses. In 1984 there were 1,221 stoppages due to strikes.

Old, heavy industries no longer seemed wanted. Some parts of the country were hit very hard in the '80s as steel plants, coal mines and factories closed down. By 1984, the number of people without a job had risen to 3.6 million.

Getting about

A traffic jam in the early '80s. How do these cars look different from today's?

Family cars of the 1980s were much boxier than today's curvier cars. More and more vehicles started to come with gadgets, such as electric windows and sunroofs. It became law to wear a seatbelt in the front of a car in 1983.

People started to worry in the 1980s about the number of cars on the roads. **Pollution** and traffic jams were a real problem. Many drivers in the '80s were using petrol containing poisonous lead, which was much more polluting than the **unleaded** fuel we use today.

TIME DIFFERENCE

The cost of petrol has rocketed since the '80s. In 1987, it was 38.4 pence per litre. Now it is over 130 pence per litre.

Cycle routes were set up in some towns and cities, to encourage more people to cycle. In 1985, inventor Sir Clive Sinclair made an electric tricycle called the 'C5'. It didn't pollute the air, but it never caught on.

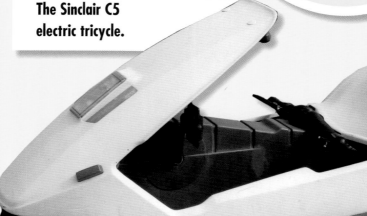

The Sinclair C5 electric tricycle.

Matty asks his dad about the car he drove:

My first car was a Vauxhall Chevette. It cost me £250 which I had saved myself from the paper round I did. It was cherry red and had a tape deck. Later on I hand-painted the wheels white to make it look very trendy.

'I hand-painted the wheels to make it look trendy.'

Sporty cars became a common luxury item for the wealthy in the '80s. Models of Porsche were very popular.

A Porsche 911 Turbo made in 1982.

Sarah asks her dad how he used to travel:

I rode a Suzuki GP100 motorbike in the '80s. It was my pride and joy. You didn't have to take any official training to ride a small motorcycle then. The man I bought it from showed me how to ride it in the car park!

High-speed railways were developed further in the 1980s. The new InterCity train could travel at 140 mph (225 kph).

An InterCity train leaves King's Cross station, London in 1988.

Holiday time

Holidays abroad became a lot more common in the 1980s as plane tickets got cheaper. Package holidays to hot countries such as Spain continued to be popular. Many people began to visit countries outside of Europe, such as the USA or Egypt.

More holidaymakers were going abroad in search of sunshine and heat.

Matty asks his dad about holidays abroad:
In 1988, we had our first foreign holiday. We went to Fuengirola in Spain. It was brilliant and really hot. We slept on the beach in the day and at night we would go to discos. I was a bit anxious about flying on a plane for the very first time.

Holidays to Spain increased as plane tickets became cheaper.

TIME DIFFERENCE

The number of people taking holidays abroad increased from 12 million in 1980 to 19 million by 1987. In the same time the number of people who had a holiday in the UK dropped from 37 million to 28 million.

British seaside resorts were struggling to attract as many visitors as they had done in the past. Some **holiday camps** had to close down. Lots of people took self-catering holidays in the UK where you rented a house for a week. For families it was often cheaper than staying in hotels.

In the '80s, more people could afford to take a second holiday in the year. Often the main holiday was a trip abroad, and a shorter mini-break was taken in the UK.

Matty's mum, Julie (left) on a holiday break near Barmouth in Wales.

Alice asks her stepsister about her holidays:

In 1983, our family took a package holiday to the Costa Brava in Spain. I particularly enjoyed being served by the handsome Spanish waiters. I also remember the massive ice creams, pedaloes, bicycles and the sun! Most of our holidays were spent in Devon or Cornwall though, where we hired a caravan or a cottage.

Here are photos of Alice's stepsister (centre) on holiday in Devon, outside her caravan and on the beach.

Find out what your family remembers

Try asking members of your family what they remember about the 1980s. You could ask them the same questions that children in this book have asked and then compare the answers you get. Ask your relatives how they think that life in the '80s was different from today. Get them to talk about their favourite memories or important events of the time. This will help you build up your own picture of life in the 1980s. It will also help you find out more about your family history.

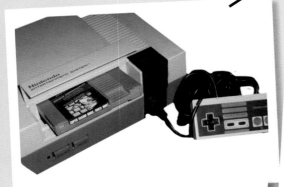

The Nintendo Entertainment System (NES) games console and *Super Mario Brothers* game cartridge.

Timeline

1980 Beatles legend John Lennon is shot dead in New York.

1981 IBM develops the first personal computers (PCs). The computer game *Pacman* is a major hit.

1982 War breaks out when Argentina invades the British-owned Falkland Islands.
Michael Jackson releases the best-selling album *Thriller*.
UK unemployment rises above 3 million.

1983 The Cabbage Patch Kids toy dolls are released.

1984 Apple Computers' first Macintosh PC goes on sale.

1985 Live Aid pop concerts raise money for Africa.
Eastenders airs for the first time.
The Nintendo Entertainment System and *Super Mario Brothers* game are launched.

1986 The Chernobyl nuclear power station in Ukraine explodes in the worst nuclear disaster of all time.

1987 Introduction of debit cards.
The Great Storm with wind speeds of over 200 kph, kills 14 people in England and brings down 15 million trees.

1988 CD singles go on sale for the first time.
A passenger plane is blown up and falls on the Scottish town of Lockerbie in the UK's worst ever terrorist attack.

1989 The Berlin Wall which divides East and West Germany is knocked down.
96 Liverpool fans die in a crush at the Hillsborough football stadium during an FA Cup semi final.

Glossary

boomed
Grew rapidly.

craze
An object or activity that becomes hugely popular for a short period of time.

credit card
A small plastic card which allows the user to buy goods on credit. To buy something on credit means you pay for it in the future.

designer clothes
Expensive clothes made by a famous fashion designer.

dinkies
Partners living together without children, in which each partner has a paid job. The 'dink' stands for double income, no kids.

fax machine
A machine that can scan a document and send it via a telephone line to another fax machine where a copy of that document can then be printed out.

ghetto blaster
A large radio with a cassette player, which could be carried on the move.

heavy metal
A type of rock music with a harsh sound and a strong beat.

hip hop
A style of pop music which contains rapping and electronic sounds.

holiday camp
A site for holidaymakers that provides accommodation, entertainment and leisure facilities.

mining
The process of digging out coal or other rocks or minerals from underground.

pollution
Damage to the air with dirty or poisonous substances.

sequel
A film or book that continues the story of an earlier one.

street cred
If you have street cred you are admired by young fashionable people.

strike
Refuse to work as a form of protest.

supercar
A powerful, fast and expensive sports car.

synthesiser
An electronic musical instrument that can produce a wide variety of sounds. It is usually operated by a keyboard.

unemployed
Without a job.

unleaded
Describes a type of petrol that does not have the soft metal, lead, added.

yuppie
A young, well paid person, who works in the city and has a luxurious lifestyle.

Further information

Books:
Growing Up in the Eighties, by Kathryn Walker, Wayland, 2002
The 1980s (Dates of a Decade), by Joseph Harris, Franklin Watts, 2009
The 1980s (I Can Remember), by Sally Hewitt, Franklin Watts, 2010

Websites:
This website has lots of memories from people who grew up in the 1980s
http://news.bbc.co.uk/1/hi/magazine/decades/1980s/
For an overview of the 1980s with links to other websites, try
http://primaryhomeworkhelp.co.uk/war/1980s.html

Index